MONSTER HUNTERS

FINDING VAMPIRES

By Bert Wilberforce

Gareth Stevens PUBLISHING

Please visit our website, www.garethstevens.com. For a free color catalog of all our high-quality books, call toll free 1-800-542-2595 or fax 1-877-542-2596.

Library of Congress Cataloging-in-Publication Data
Names: Wilberforce, Bert, author.
Title: Finding vampires / Bert Wilberforce.
Description: Buffalo, N.Y. : Gareth Stevens Publishing, 2026. | Series: Monster hunters | Includes index.
Identifiers: LCCN 2024056802 (print) | LCCN 2024056803 (ebook) | ISBN 9781482472172 (library binding) | ISBN 9781482472165 (paperback) | ISBN 9781482472189 (ebook)
Subjects: LCSH: Vampires–Juvenile literature. | Europe–Geography–Juvenile literature.
Classification: LCC GR830.V3 W49 2026 (print) | LCC GR830.V3 (ebook) | DDC 398.210094–dc23/eng/20250107
LC record available at https://lccn.loc.gov/2024056802
LC ebook record available at https://lccn.loc.gov/2024056803

Published in 2026 by
Gareth Stevens Publishing
2544 Clinton Street
Buffalo, NY 14224

Designer: Andrea Davison-Bartolotta
Editor: Therese Shea

Photo credits: Cover, pp. 1, 19 Shutterstock AI/Shutterstock.com; cover, p. 1, series art (glowing compass rose) LoveDesignShop/Shutterstock.com; series art (cardinal compass rose) Angela Ksen/Shutterstock.com; series art (ordinal compass rose) jame05/Shutterstock.com; series art (fact box rope border) LanaN/Shutterstock.com; series art (fact box wood) EE SPACE/Shutterstock.com; series art (map background) Olha Andreichyn/Shutterstock.com; series art (curled paper background) MIGUEL G. SAAVEDRA/Shutterstock.com; series art (flat paper) Paladin12/Shutterstock.com; p. 4 ArshadBusro/Shutterstock.com; p. 5 (graphic organizer) Dmitry Natashin/Shutterstock.com; p. 5 (main) Studio Romantic/Shutterstock.com; p. 7 (background) Sodel Vladyslav/Shutterstock.com; pp. 7, 9, 13, 17, 19 (map) Peter Hermes Furian/Shutterstock.com; p. 9 (bottom) Nitikan T/Shutterstock.com; p. 11 (map) Flappiefh/ File:1346-1353 spread of the Black Death in Europe map.svg/Wikimedia Commons; p. 11 (inset) File:DoutieIt3.jpg/Wikimedia Commons; p. 11 (plague doctor) Refluo/Shutterstock.com; p. 13 (bottom) File:Vlad Tepes, the Impaler, Prince of Wallachia (1456-1462) (died 1477).jpg/Wikimedia Commons; p. 15 (main) Science History Images/Alamy Stock Photo; pp. 15, 27 (background) Kjpargeter/Shutterstock.com; p. 15 (hands) Vector Tradition/Shutterstock.com; p. 17 (bottom) SCStock/Shutterstock.com; p. 20 Rainer Lesniewski/Shutterstock.com; p. 21 (grave) Cbarry123/File:MercyBrownGravestone (bearb Sp).jpg/Wikimedia Commons; p. 21 (ad) File:Believe in Vampires.png/Wikimedia Commons; p. 23 (bottom) Benny Marty/Shutterstock.com; p. 23 (map) Serban Bogdan/Shutterstock.com; p. 25 (inset) RYLex/Shutterstock.com; p. 25 (main) VIAVAL TOURS/Shutterstock.com; p. 27 belizar/Shutterstock.com; pp. 28, 29 (map) Janos Levente/Shutterstock.com; pp. 28, 29 (paper) AKaiser/Shutterstock.com.

Printed in the United States of America

CPSIA compliance information: Batch #CSGS26: For further information contact Gareth Stevens at 1-800-542-2595.

CONTENTS

Words in the glossary appear in **bold** type the first time they are used in the text.

VAMPIRE HUNT!

Imagine you're invited to a party on your street. You don't see this neighbor much. He says he goes to night school. When he answers the door, he gives you a smile. He has two *really* pointy teeth. He's also wearing a cape. In his living room, he has . . . a **coffin**? Ok, get out of there—your neighbor is a vampire!

In this book, you'll travel much farther than down your street looking for vampire tales. Pack maps to find your way!

People have told stories of vampire-like creatures for hundreds of years. Today, vampire **costumes** are popular on Halloween too.

Vampire stories are all different, but these are some common features of these spooky monsters.

COMMON VAMPIRE FEATURES

- Drain people's blood with sharp teeth called fangs
- Can turn other people into vampires
- Weakened by sunlight
- Can turn into a bat
- Have great strength
- Can't be seen in a mirror
- Don't have a shadow
- Can control their victims' minds

GET TO GREECE

Let's start the vampire hunt in Greece. Look at the map of the **continent** of Europe. You can find the country of Greece using a compass rose. This is the tool on a map that shows the four main directions: north (N), south (S), east (E), and west (W). These are called the cardinal directions. Greece is in southern Europe. Do you see it?

Ancient Greek tales tell of creatures that sucked blood out of sleeping people's bodies. Scary!

BEHIND THE MYTH

Ancient Greek vampire monsters weren't much like the vampires of movies today. Some were said to be ghosts and others had hair of fire.

Greece has the longest coastline of any country touching the Mediterranean Sea. It has about 2,000 islands!

GRAVE PROOF

Head northeast from Greece to Bulgaria for proof that people believed in the old tales of vampires. Scientists have found odd things in graveyards that suggest people were trying to stop the dead from rising. For example, in the town of Sozopol in Bulgaria, they found 700-year-old skeletons with teeth removed and iron stakes, or rods, pinning them down.

More than 100 "vampire skeletons" have been found in Bulgaria alone. Many of the most famous vampire tales are from this area of Europe.

Bulgaria is on the Balkan **Peninsula** in southern Europe. On this compass rose, you can see directions exactly between the cardinal directions. These are the ordinal directions: northeast (NE), southeast (SE), northwest (NW), and southwest (SW).

Behind the Myth

People who were disliked or thought to be evil in real life were often those who were believed to be vampires after their death.

THE BLACK DEATH

Vampire tales and disease, or illness, were linked during the **Middle Ages** in many parts of Europe. **Plague** sometimes killed whole communities. People didn't understand how diseases spread from person to person at that time. Blaming vampires was one way to make sense of death and disease.

A widespread plague in the mid-1300s was so deadly it was called the Black Death. Among the symptoms, or signs, of the disease were black skin spots called boils that oozed blood and pus. About 20 million people died of the Black Death across Europe.

Behind the Myth

Some victims of the Black Death coughed up blood. That led people to think they were vampires drinking the blood of others!

In this image, people bury victims of the plague. Sometimes stones were placed in the mouths of the dead so they couldn't suck blood if they rose as "undead" vampires.

This is a map showing the spread of the Black Death across Europe. Map keys can help you understand facts on a map. This map's key tells you certain colors stand for certain years.

VLAD THE IMPALER

Many vampire tales today are based on a book called *Dracula*. It was written in 1897 by Irish author Bram Stoker. The book is about a blood-sucking vampire named Count Dracula. He lived in a castle in a place called Transylvania.

Transylvania is a real area of today's Romania, a country in southeastern Europe. The main character of Dracula may have been based in part on an actual person who lived in Romania. Vlad the Impaler was a cruel prince there in the 1400s.

Romania is a mountainous country north of Bulgaria. It also shares borders with Serbia, Hungary, Ukraine, and Moldova. It has a coastline on the Black Sea to the southeast.

Vlad the Impaler was the son of Vlad II Dracul ("dragon"), so he was called Vlad Dracula ("son of the dragon").

Vlad Dracula was born in Transylvania, but he was a prince of Wallachia, a **principality** south of Transylvania. Vlad became known for the cruel way he treated his enemies. In 1462, he ordered that his enemies be **impaled** on tall stakes. This was a warning to others not to fight him. It's how he got his nickname, "Impaler."

Some records say that Vlad dipped his bread in his enemies' blood as another scary warning. Bram Stoker may have taken the name Dracula from Vlad, knowing about his terrible deeds.

BEHIND THE MYTH

Some scientists think Vlad Dracula may have had a condition in which he cried tears of blood!

In this 1499 German artwork, Vlad Dracula eats near his impaled enemies. Some think he killed about 80,000 people in all!

DRACULA'S CASTLE

Today, one of the biggest draws for visitors to Romania is Bran Castle in Transylvania. It's nicknamed Dracula's Castle. However, Vlad Dracula didn't have land in Transylvania, so this castle has little to do with him. (He may have been held prisoner there for a time, though.)

Some think the castle, which stands high in the Carpathian Mountains, was the model for Dracula's castle in Bram Stoker's book. Stoker never visited Transylvania, though it seems likely from the account of the castle in the book that he read about it.

Bran Castle is in central Romania. It's northwest of the capital city of Bucharest.

Bran Castle was completed in 1388 to stop enemies from crossing into Transylvania.

SERBIA'S SCARY STORIES

After the Middle Ages, vampire tales continued to spread. Head west to the town of Vojvodina in today's Serbia. Early 1700s records say villagers there complained about vampires causing deaths in their community. Doctors didn't believe them but allowed the dead to be dug up. Some of the dead had blood on their faces!

This blood was likely just a sign of disease or the aftereffects of death, but villagers thought it proved they were vampires. Newspapers printed these stories—and spread the fear of vampires.

Serbia is another country on the Balkan Peninsula. Vojvodina, Serbia, is west of Bran Castle in Romania. Check the compass rose.

Behind the Myth

Some of the tales of vampires being "undead" may have come about because back then, it was hard to know when people were truly dead. People who regained **consciousness** after illness may have been accused of being undead.

MERCY BROWN

Head west from Europe to the continent of North America for another true tale. Mercy Brown lived on a farm in Exeter, Rhode Island, in the 1800s. Mercy and many of her family members died of an illness called tuberculosis. But some in the community didn't think it was disease that was killing people.

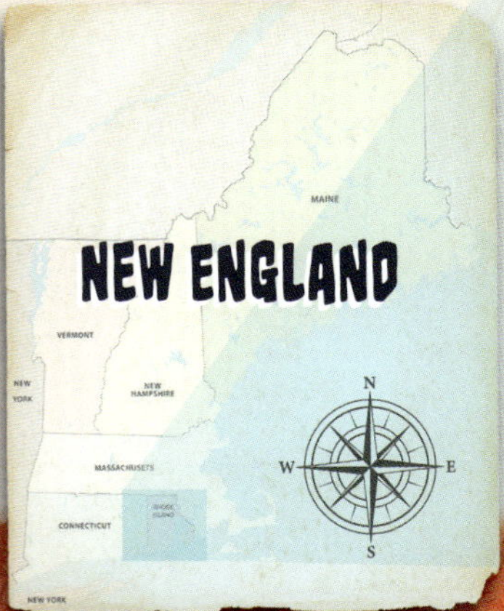

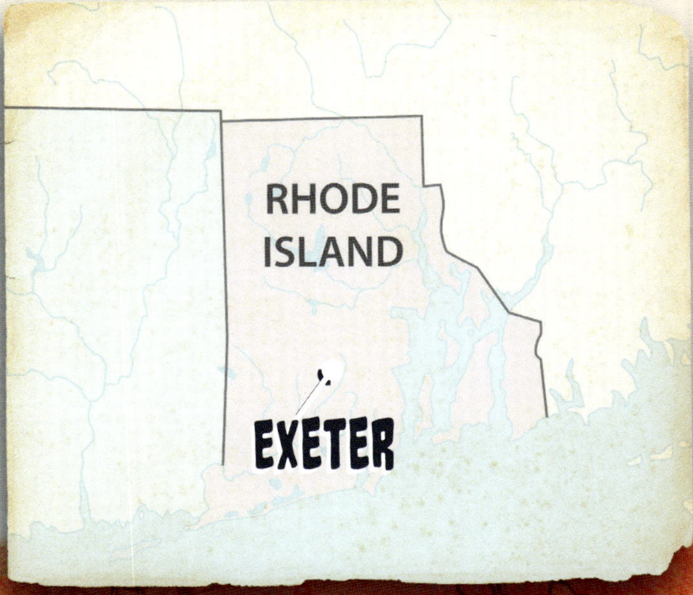

They dug up buried members of the Brown family. They thought Mercy was a vampire because her body was well preserved, or in good condition. They performed **rituals** to stop Mercy from becoming a vampire. Unsurprisingly, others still died of tuberculosis.

BELIEVE IN VAMPIRES.

Rhode Islanders Who Are Sure That They Do Exist.

Instances Told of Where the Living Have Been Attacked and Preyed Upon by These Representatives of an Unseen World.

A MEMBER OF THE ANTI-VAMPIRE PARTY.

The story of Mercy Brown was during a time when many people in New England had a great fear of vampires.

Behind the Myth

Mercy Brown's body was likely well preserved because she was buried during the cold winter. But people didn't understand much about the science behind death in those days.

PERUVIAN TALE

Not all vampire stories are from long ago. Travel south to Peru, a country in western South America. In 1993, hundreds of people gathered near the coffin of Sarah Ellen Roberts, nicknamed the Bride of Dracula, in the town of Pisco.

Roberts had been killed for witchcraft in England in 1913. Some thought she was a vampire too. It was said that Roberts promised to rise from the dead 80 years later. However, the grave watchers of 1993 were disappointed. No one came out of Roberts's coffin.

Pisco is in southern Peru, on the Pacific coast. It's directly south of Exeter, Rhode Island.

Behind the Myth

According to the tale, Sarah Ellen Roberts wasn't permitted to be buried in England. Her husband was allowed to bury her in Pisco, Peru, however.

VAMPIRES STILL IN STYLE

Head home to continue your hunt for vampire tales! Why? The tales are still being told in today's books, movies, and TV shows. Some stories are based on famous tales, such as *Dracula*. Others have their own spin on vampires, such as the *Twilight* books and movies.

Still others create vampires that are less scary and more kid-friendly. You might have noticed the funny vampire in the LEGO movies and TV shows. And perhaps you grew up watching and learning from Count von Count, the counting vampire muppet on *Sesame Street*!

Keep your eyes open, and you'll see many examples of vampires in popular **culture.**

COUNT VON COUNT

VAMPIRE MYSTERIES SOLVED?

So, do you believe in vampires? Many people don't. They say vampire tales reveal, or tell us, how much people didn't understand about their world. In fact, modern science has solved at least some vampire-related mysteries.

For example, in many tales, sunlight harms vampires, so they only come out at night. But in real life, some people have skin conditions called porphyria, which cause a **sensitivity** to sunlight. One kind also explains why some people have longer, sharper teeth than others.

Behind the Myth

Rabies is a disease that can cause people to want to bite other people in some bad cases. Some people with rabies were likely thought to be vampires.

Vampire bats feed mostly on the blood of large animals, such as cattle. They were named after the vampires of the tales and later appeared in vampire books, including Bram Stoker's *Dracula*.

VAMPIRE STORIES SPOTTED!

There are many tales of vampire creatures around the world. Continue your journey to learn more!
Transylvania—Dracula's Castle, otherwise known as Bran Castle, is found here.
Wallachia—Vlad Dracula was a cruel ruler here in the 1400s.
Sozopol, Bulgaria—Graves of suspected vampires were found here.
Vojvodina, Serbia—People blamed vampires for spreading disease here.
Greece—Ancient tales of blood-sucking monsters began here.
N
W
E
S

GLOSSARY

coffin: A box in which a dead person is buried.

consciousness: The state of being able to see, hear, or sense what is happening.

continent: One of Earth's seven great landmasses.

costume: Clothes worn by someone who is trying to look like another person or thing.

culture: The arts and other ways of life of a group of people.

impale: To cause a pointed object to go into or through something or someone.

Middle Ages: A time in European history from about 500 to 1500.

peninsula: A narrow piece of land that extends into water from the mainland.

plague: A fast-spreading disease that causes death to many people.

principality: An area that is ruled by a prince.

ritual: A formal ceremony.

sensitivity: Easily affected or even harmed by something.

FOR MORE INFORMATION

Books

Novak, Sara. *The Genius Kid's Guide to Mythical Creatures*. Mendota Heights, MN: North Star Kids, 2023.

Watt, E. Melanie. *Vampire Bats*. New York, NY: Lightbox Learning, 2024.

Williams, Heather DiLorenzo. *Vampire*. Fremont, CA: Full Tilt Press, 2022.

Websites

Vampire
kids.britannica.com/kids/article/vampire/600681
Read more about vampire stories' origins and more.

Vampire Bats vs. Vampires!
www.beardsleyzoo.org/blog/vampire-bats-vs-vampires
Learn about vampire bats and their link to vampire legends.

INDEX